What Do You Have To Say?
Poetry's Eternal Question

What Do You Have To Say?
Poetry's Eternal Question

*Poems about Knowledge, Heart, Mind,
Truth, Caring, Conflict*

S T Kimbrough, Jr.

FOREWORD BY
J. Richard Watson

RESOURCE *Publications* · Eugene, Oregon

WHAT DO YOU HAVE TO SAY? POETRY'S ETERNAL QUESTION
Poems about Knowledge, Heart, Mind, Truth, Caring, Conflict

Copyright © 2024 S T Kimbrough, Jr. All rights reserved. Except for brief quotations in critical publications or reviews, no part of this book may be reproduced in any manner without prior written permission from the publisher. Write: Permissions, Wipf and Stock Publishers, 199 W. 8th Ave., Suite 3, Eugene, OR 97401.

Resource Publications
An Imprint of Wipf and Stock Publishers
199 W. 8th Ave., Suite 3
Eugene, OR 97401

www.wipfandstock.com

PAPERBACK ISBN: 979-8-3852-1396-2
HARDCOVER ISBN: 979-8-3852-1397-9
EBOOK ISBN: 979-8-3852-1398-6

02/28/24

Contents

Foreword by J. Richard Watson   ix
Introduction   xiii

SECTION 1. What Do You Have to Say about What You Say?

1. Learn Your Language Well	3
2. What Did You Say?	5
3. The Art of Words	6
4. One New Word Each Day	7
5. The Power of Words	8
6. Words 1	10
7. Words 2	11
8. A Common Language	12
9. Unspoken Words	13
10. Silence	14

SECTION 2. What Do You Have to Say about Knowledge?

11. I Really Don't Know	17
12. Knowledge and Reason	18
13. Some People Think Too Much	19
14. Innocent Simplicity	20
15. Certainty of Knowledge	21
16. Certainty?	22
17. Reality?	23

SECTION 3. What Do You Have to Say about Matters of the Heart and Mind?

18. Mind and Heart	27
19. Moods	28
20. Decisions	29
21. Day Dreaming	30
22. Winnowing	31
23. Poetry	32
24. Creative Sensitivity	33
25. Alive Emotions	34
26. Whence Happiness?	35
27. Human Loss	37

SECTION 4. What Do You Have to Say about Truth?

28. Truth	41
29. Persistent Truth	42
30. If Truth Be Told	43
31. Truth Détente	44
32. The Art of Lying	45
33. Dishonesty's Long Game	47
34. Narcissism Is Alive and Well	48
35. Truth and Grace	49
36. Misunderstandings	50

SECTION 5. What Do You Have to Say about Caring?

37. Who Cares?	53
38. My Choice	54
39. Be Thankful	55

40. Loneliness	56
41. Right and Wrong	57
42. First Things First	59
43. Worn Sad	60
44. No Change	61
45. Ingratitude	63
46. Composure	64
47. Desires	65
48. If Love is There	66
49. Love's Measure	67
50. Practice Patience, Master Fear	68
51. A Human Curse?	70

SECTION 6. What Do You Have to Say about Conflict?

52. U.S. Farm Workers	75
53. Economy and Poverty	77
54. A Daily Struggle	78
55. Conflict	79
56. A Sheltered Past	81
57. Conversion	83
58. Do Unto Others—What?	85
59. In Birmingham	87
60. Justice and Mercy	89
61. Lost Humanity?	90
62. Which Way Humankind?	92
63. Equality & Justice for All	93
Index of Subjects and Names	97

Foreword

"Words, words, words." It was Hamlet's reply to Polonius, who had only asked politely, as anyone might, "What do you read, my Lord?" Hamlet's rude response makes the listener wonder, for it reveals so much in its refusal to reveal anything—that Hamlet is a disturbed young man (for good reason), who is capable of delivering an unpleasant brush-off, that he thinks Polonius is an old fool, that Polonius is a tedious nuisance. The thrice-repeated word tells us nothing, and yet it tells us a great deal. What words tell us about ourselves and others, and about the state of the world, is the subject of this book.

S T Kimbrough's latest collection of poems is full of questions about words, how we express ourselves, how we communicate, and what this tells us about ourselves and our society. This volume begins light-heartedly, with questions about literary convention: "Do I say 'if I were' or 'was'?" Should it be "may I?" or "can I?" But spelling, and conventional literacy, become important. They can be a way by which we are judged as acceptable, or not: "How do you spell 'ciborium'?" Words, as we know from daily use, often tell us more about ourselves than we would like others to know. Class distinction, for instance, is registered in many novels and poems by the way in which words are used: "The 'eathen in' is blindness bows down to wood an' stone" is a parody of a well-known hymn, "From Greenland's icy mountains," but it is also Kipling's way of telling the reader that the speaker is not officer class. Less obviously, the words that we speak or write are evidence of our character and inclinations. And words are persuasive: if we accept them unquestioningly, they can control our lives, as politicians know.

Words can be played with, too, in ways that give delight. Kimbrough has a poem in this first section that orders rhymes about as if they were soldiers: perceptibility / culpability / imbecility / reliability / respectability / liability / instability / civility. But such delight gives way to seriousness, as the poem ends with the need to respect others, with humility, and with the need to be sensitive. This collection moves similarly from a set of poems, sometimes even light-hearted, through a series of stages, to a profoundly moral view of the situation in which humanity finds itself.

We need words. One poem reminds us that body language can be powerful, but its range is limited; another suggests that silence is divine (but cannot take us forward). Both of these are found at the end of Section 1. Thereafter the collection steadily deepens into observation about human behavior. Section 2 is concerned with knowledge, which is affected by the ways in which we think: "Some people think too much / about themselves": narcissism leaves no room for empathy. The poem "Mind and Heart" leads into Section 3, "What do you have to say about matters of the heart and mind?" The answer is that heart and mind need to go together. Here Kimbrough, a distinguished Charles Wesley scholar, may be drawing on that great hymn-writer's insistence on the importance of the heart. If heart and mind are not together, problems follow. When they are in accord, they provide a basis for our discriminations and our beliefs, which depend in part on our memories: a key poem in this section, "Alive Emotions," describes how emotions of the mind and heart are transitory, but are retained in the storehouse of the mind.

"Truth," the subject of Section 4, takes us back to the importance of words. Dishonesty, the perpetuation of "misunderstandings" (the word begins every stanza of one poem) is part of the pattern that emerges when truth is under threat. The hope is in the old Latin phrase, *Temporis veritas filia*—truth is the daughter of time; but it has many enemies—narcissism, selfishness, strong desires, the refusal to see any point of view but one's own. The hope lies in "Caring," the subject of the next section (5): patience and love are essential to counter the forces of evil and corruption. These are displayed openly in the final part of the book, "What do you have to say about conflict?"

"Conflict" is a powerful word. It means not only war, but inequality and racial prejudice. In Section 6, Kimbrough draws vividly on his own experience as a child and young man in Alabama, brought up in a time of racial segregation and casual brutality. Birmingham, Alabama, features in his memory, and all the theories of the earlier parts of this book give way to the "I" of the author's own consciousness. It includes a poem about Alabama's prisons, "Lost humanity." That word "humanity" dominates this section, and, in retrospect, the whole book; for, as Robert Burns knew, and Kimbrough knows, "Man's inhumanity to man / Makes countless thousands mourn."

If this makes the book sound depressing, the depression leads to realism, a confrontation with the forces of evil that is itself heroic. The realism is linked to hope, which is evident in the very writing of these pieces. "We humans struggle year on year" is how one poem in the final part begins. In it Kimbrough is describing the struggle to survive for lack of food, for ill health, and for homelessness; but there is another struggle, the attempt, vital if the human race is to survive, to put humanity's trust in unselfishness, benevolence, insight, and love, in spite of everything that denies these things—lies, deceptions, words used to encourage violence and hatred, greed, the lust for power.

That is the lasting impression that is found in this book. "If a way to the Better there be, / It exacts a full look at the Worst," as Thomas Hardy wrote ("In Tenebris"). By writing these poems, Kimbrough has raised a flag in the struggle for a better world.

J. Richard Watson
Emeritus Professor of English,
University of Durham, UK

Introduction

A poem shapes words in such a way that they say something about something. Poets put their words together in many different ways from culture to culture. The choice of words, rhyme, free verse, etc., and many other aspects of composition comprise the poet's art of rhetoric. There are three main classic devices of tropes, figures, and fine turns. Certainly metaphors are one of the most well used tropes. Repetitions of words and phrases within a sentence are known as *epizeuzis*. One particular form of repetition, beginning and ending a line with the same word, is *epanadiplosis*. One may also repeat a phrase in the middle of successive sentences. This is *mesodiplosis*. To repeat a phrase in reverse order is called *antistrophe*. These are just a few rhetorical devices, and many others may be used in metrical or free verse, although rhyme, except for internal rhyme, is not necessarily as intentional in free verse as in metrical forms. In metrical verse there are many rhetorical devices which emerge from the meters themselves, be they iambic, trochaic, etc.

It is not the purpose here to pursue an extensive discussion of the characteristics of poetic rhetoric, but rather to emphasize at the outset that poetry possesses many characteristics through which it conveys meaning. Therefore, the choice of words is an essential aspect of creating the effectiveness of poetry. "Poetry is sometimes described as the compromise between the demands of a regular adherence to a metrical form and the opposing urge of a mind fired by strong emotions. True poetry is the result of extreme tension. Without the discipline of metre the emotion might be expressed in lyrical prose; without the emotion it would remain an exercise in verse."[1]

---

1. Frank Baker, *Charles Wesley's Verse, An Introduction.* (London: Epworth, 1964), 103.

INTRODUCTION

The first section, "What Do You Have To Say?" addresses the choice of words, which in itself is an art. How words are chosen by the poet is determinative for meaning, style, and flow of the narrative or theme. Obviously, there are various levels of poetic art. Some may seem, indeed be, more sophisticated in terms of grammar and syntax, but

> You need not be a Cicero,
>   a Shakespeare or a Keats;
> but learn your language well, you'll know
>   that ignorance it defeats.

Words have an unusual power and control much of our lives, whether in writing, reading, listening, or speaking. Friendly words make friends, while angry ones can lose them.

> Words, words control all of our lives,
>   believe it as we will.
> They comfort us or pierce like knives,
>   our souls with love can fill.

Words can "change perceptibility / of human culpability"; on the other hand they can "change hatred to humility, / speak words of sensitivity." It behooves human beings to think carefully of what they say. Sometimes we have no idea of the effect of our words on others.

> Our words we may leave suspended,
>   but muted they'll not be.
> We may find they've life upended;
>   we wait, we wait to see.

There are also "Unspoken Words" activated by gestures, looks, poses, and touch. "Our bodies speak without a word; / they can be wondrous, though unheard."

> When nothing's said, much more is said,
>   for silence shapes the mind.
> When nothing's said, the mind is fed,
>   with thoughts it's intertwined.

INTRODUCTION

Section 2 is titled "What Do You Have to Say About Knowledge?" Knowledge is intimately related to what we know about words, for they are interrelated. Words can shape the core of knowledge, its content, how we shape it, digest it, record it, and communicate it. If we go back in history to the development of alphabets we will find subsequently humans developing knowledge about diverse subjects. In Kramer's interesting volume *History Begins at Sumer*[2] there are early texts of commerce, medicine, literature, and a variety of other subjects. Knowledge emerges from the human ability to utilize word formation to express growing understanding of science, education, literature, etc.

> Through knowledge each child's mind expands,
> each learns of cultures, other lands.
> As children learn to add, write, read,
> their mother tongue meets a new need.
> They speak and they communicate;
> they learn with others to relate.

There is always the temptation to emphasize the expansion of the mind at the expense of expanding the understanding of the heart. Easily one falls prey to the notion that what the mind absorbs is much more important than what the heart takes in and gives. Then knowledge seated in the brain is more important than emotion and feeling. To know and to feel tend to become opposing tendencies.

> To educate the mind alone
>   and to forget the heart
> will penalize you when you're grown
>   and tear your life apart.
>
> The heart needs education too,
>   its sensitivities
> need careful guidance through and through,
>   no liabilities.

---

2. Samuel Noah Kramer, *History Begins at Sumer*. (New York: Doubleday Books, 1959).

INTRODUCTION

The heart and mind go hand in hand,
  there's knowledge that both need.
With both you'll better understand,
  therefore make this your creed:

Let mind and heart together grow
  in knowledge, and be free,
and make all those around you know
  a sweet philanthropy.

Section 3 has the title "What Do You Have to Say About Truth?" Truth is directly related to our use of words and to knowledge, for how we shape what we say with words determines how we understand, know, and communicate knowledge. Words are used to state the truth, explain the truth, and/or disguise the truth. Without words our knowledge is greatly inhibited, and so is our ability to imbibe it and to share it. What constitutes the truth, however, has become questionable today for those endorsing alternative facts, or for those who endorse truth by repetition.

For repetition is today
  The origin of "truth."
The truth becomes what you might say;
  objection is uncouth.

If someone says, "Tell me the truth,"
  what answer might you get?
What you were taught in prime of youth:
  "Truth should not facts forget"?

A primary opponent of truth is the lie. "Though truth endures and never dies, / it struggles constantly with lies."

The fact is this: truth never wins,
  if one thinks truth and lies are twins.

Lying for many is an art, and it is done artfully. Sometimes lies are so artfully conceived and eloquently expressed that untruth appears to be the truth.

INTRODUCTION

> The art of lying with finesse
>   through centuries has grown
> till now we sadly ask, confess:
>   Can true or false be known?

Section 4 is titled "What Do You Have to Say About Caring?" This quite naturally follows a knowledge of the mind and heart, which can develop in us a sense of caring. Knowledge seated solely in the mind may find it difficult to care to others and their needs, particularly for those who are less fortunate, illiterate or poorly educated, mentally and physically challenged.

We choose to care or not to care. "Careless, caring, or care-free, / which one would I like to be?"

> If I'm careless, I don't care;
> if I care, then I'm aware
> that I should care for others,
> who are my sisters, brothers.

It is not always simple and natural to be a caring person. Do I want the poor really to have a chance to share in the abundance of life?

> Be thankful if life's circumstance
> gives those in poverty a chance.
> Be thankful if I have been blessed,
> if I can help those who're distressed.

It is rather easy to think, however, that this simply means distributing our resources to those less privileged. But human beings have many other resources that they often fail to share. Those who are destitute and without the simplest resources of life can benefit from who they are, not just what they have.

> The first step is to BE a friend;
>   most surely this is no surprise
> that friendship you cannot pretend;
>   to BE a friend shows you are wise.

We all face the question: What do we really want? What do we desire above all else? How do we answer this question for ourselves?

INTRODUCTION

> Desires need genuine concern
> the needs of others to discern.
> For only when we see beyond
> ourselves and things of which we're fond
> will we control our strong desires,
> as our humanity requires.

For most persons self-desire and self-love are not difficult. It is very easy to think of oneself first. All self-concern is not a disadvantage. Self-esteem is important for every human being. Somewhere amid these concerns, there needs to be a spark of love—of self and of others.

But love's meaning is so elusive, yet it gives life to the living.

> Love rules emotions and the heart;
> it's sensed in every sinew, part.
> Our minds it also captivates,
> unspoken thoughts it dominates.
> Love's measure has no measure, hence
> its meaning we cannot condense.

Unquestionably both patience and fear make it difficult for us to love as we should. Therefore,

> To practice patience, master fear:
>   beyond yourself begin
> to think of others and adhere
>   to love of self within.

Section 5 bears the title "What Do You Have to Say About Social Issues?" and addresses how what we have to say about what we say, and what we say about knowledge and caring relate to how we relate to the world around us. Living in a vacuum within ourselves is not an option. So, I ask myself: Am I willing to think of those of whom I usually may not think?

> I looked across a field today
>   to see farm workers at their toil.
> The sun was hot and fields of hay
>   so steamed with heat as if to boil.

INTRODUCTION

How can I respond to them with integrity?

> Treat them with honor, dignity,
>   their language, culture dignify.
> For them act with impunity;
>   this U.S. farms can justify!

So many of the hardest laborers are the poorest. Yet they provide the means whereby food is delivered to our tables. The poor are not just African Americans, though many of them are poor, but Appalachia, for example, is still filled with a huge poverty-stricken, white population. Some of them suffer from the loss of income because of closed coal mines where they were poorly paid before the closings. The ever-growing Hispanic population, on which agriculture has become very dependent in the U.S.A., struggles to rise above the poverty level.

> Economy and poverty
>   seem to go hand in hand,
> and poor folk face adversity
>   in every global land.

> Consumer-planned economy
>   based on supply-demand
> can give the rich autonomy,
>   the poor an empty hand.

Having grown up in the deep south, I learned that racism was a problem that could not be avoided, at least according to what my parents had taught me.

> This conflict is like no other,
>   for Christ's words, I'd been taught:
> you are to "love one another,"
>   if you'd live as you ought.

> Did Christians really this believe,
>   I wondered: Can this be?
> For Christ said, "I will *all* receive,"
>   and then said, "Follow me."

INTRODUCTION

I recall that every morning at the beginning of the school day the students of our completely segregated school were asked to repeat the Pledge of Allegiance to the U.S. flag.

> Our school was white, no blacks allowed,
>   and our school day began
> with prayer when all our heads were bowed,
>   as if all were God's plan.
>
> We pledged allegiance to our flag,
>   some with a southern drawl;
> I later knew the troubling snag:
>   we said, "justice for all."

The poems here do not solve problems but are a call to alarm that what we have to say greatly impacts the choices that we make personally and that communities make corporately. Think carefully about what you have to say about anything, especially the gravest and most significant concerns of life.

SECTION 1

What Do You Have to Say about What You Say?

1. Learn Your Language Well

Each day I wrestle more and more
    with English-language speech:
are sentence diagrams a bore,
    subjunctives a gross breach,
a breach of English that I learned
    when I first went to school?
But now if I'm one that's concerned
    with words, am I a fool?

Do I say "if I were" or "was"?
    Which is correct or right?
Does sentence context give me pause?
    Who cares what I may write?
Do I say "may I" or "can I"?
    Who really, really cares?
How will this help me to get by
    with all of my affairs?

Syntax and grammar are just fine
    for ivory-tower folk,
who worship at a language shrine.
    Some think they are a joke.
Yet orators, masters of speech,
    have saved many a day
from war, dissension, for they teach
    with words a better way.

Their eloquence in their own tongue,
    their mast'ry of each word,
they learned at first when they were young:
    such mast'ry's not absurd.
You need not be a Cicero,
    a Shakespeare or a Keats.
But learn your language well, you'll know
    that ignorance it defeats.

2. What Did You Say?

When words sound like we know it all,
    no doubt we've thought it so.
Conceit delights to shock, appall
    with "O, you didn't know?"

We need to think humility,
    admit when we are wrong.
It's central to civility;
    when humble, we are strong.

If we control words each to each,
    prevent all wrong intent,
and use humility in speech,
    our converse is well spent.

3. The Art of Words

My grandfather learned a new word
    each day, so I've been told.
Perhaps he thought this act deterred
    or slowed his growing old.

Pronunciation was an art
    grandfather knew quite well.
"Ode to the West Wind" learned by heart,
    his rend'ring cast a spell.

A radio station asked him
    to broadcast Shelley's lines.
He spoke as though they were a hymn
    that words with art combines.

Would that the art of words we saw
    as my grandfather did.
Then Shelley's words we'd hear in awe;
    their art would not be hid.

4. One New Word Each Day

A task for stay-at-homers now,
    if English is their daily tongue:
each day learn a new word somehow,
    good practice for the old and young.

How do you spell "ciborium"?
    Does "carrot" have two r's?
And what about "haustorium"?
    Can you name twenty stars?

The English language is stocked full
    of words you do not know.
You know that you can "shoot the bull,"
    but language skills can grow.

Just daily learn a single word,
    a word you've never known.
Let others think you quite absurd,
    but leave them well alone.

5. The Power of Words

We babble sounds after we're born,
    no one knows what we say.
We make the sounds in early morn
    and then throughout the day.
We ooh and aah, goo goo, and cry,
    our moms know what we say.
They hold us close, and they know why,
    that's where we like to stay.

We learn to say papa, mama;
    we learn our ABCs.
We read and write, what a drama;
    sometimes school work's a breeze?
We go to college, graduate school;
    we earn a Ph.D.
Our parents know we're not a fool,
    for words, words are the key.

Our first sounds have come very far
    from early babble sounds.
Our words tell others who we are;
    our words set many bounds
of openness or prejudice,
    of truth, dishonesty,
of bravery or cowardice
    or simple decency.

What language do we learn at first?
    Just one or are there more?
The main thing is we have a thirst
    to use words that will store
up friendship and kindness for all,
    respect and dignity.
Our words may calm or cause cabal,
    bring peace, calamity.

Words, words control all of our lives,
    believe it as we will.
They comfort us or pierce like knives,
    or souls with love can fill.
Today take care each word you say,
    for lives hang on each word,
lest others openly should say:
    "Your life, your life's absurd!"

6. Words 1

To write, to speak, communicate
are gifts we should appreciate,
and yet all three can complicate,
can desecrate or consecrate.

How do we learn to use these three
to be the best that we can be,
to learn how amiability
leads to agreeability?

Words change perceptibility
of human culpability
through lying's imbecility
or truth's reliability.

When lost respectability
becomes a liability,
evokes gross instability,
there is no more civility.

Change hatred to humility,
speak words of sensitivity;
respect the capability
of everyone's ability.

7. Words 2

The words that one suspends in time
    in poetry or prose
suggest reality sublime,
    which often no one knows.

The words indeed are suspensions
    in sentence or in rhyme
of truths, perhaps apprehensions,
    of now or any time.

Our words we may leave suspended,
    but muted they'll not be.
We may find they've life upended;
    we wait, we wait to see.

8. A Common Language

There's innocence with which we're born;
we waken with it every morn.
When do we lose it? Tell me why
each child on earth has no reply.
Both hate and prejudice they learn
from those who with vile anger burn.
Each infant does not have a choice,
each one is born with the same voice:
The language of the "hunger cry"
is spoken in New York, Mumbai.
So when we're born we're all alike
until just like a lightning strike
we learn to speak in different tongues
and words burst forth from heaving lungs.
We speak of love, we speak of hate,
our words caress, our words berate.
We may of love or hatred speak,
of pride, of greed, or of the meek.
Alike when we are born and die,
we have one language: "hunger cry."
We have a great and urgent need,
a need for which each one should plead—
between our birth and death to find
a language of at least like mind
to urge, with words from heart and mind,
humanity its worth to find.

9. Unspoken Words

Our bodies speak without a word,
which makes us wonder what is heard:
an open hand ready to aid,
or folded hands when one has prayed;
a smile that greets a broken heart
and stops a tear lest it should start;
the open arms that welcome one,
who was for years a long-lost son;
a frown that quickly can refuse
another's efforts to abuse;
a handshake's hospitality,
a soft touch with gentility;
a love enriched by warm embrace,
a look of joy on someone's face;
our bodies speak without a word;
they can be wondrous, though unheard.

10. Silence

When nothing's said, much more is said,
    for silence shapes the mind.
When nothing's said, the mind is fed,
    with thoughts it's intertwined.

"Say nothing": often sound advice;
    in silence think things through.
Our speech will then be more precise.
    We'll know how our thoughts grew.

In silence we can think and pray,
    and let our thoughts refine;
and live a quiet, thoughtful day,
    for silence is divine.

SECTION 2

What Do You Have to Say about Knowledge?

11. I Really Don't Know

What constitutes a miracle,
or is this word satirical
for those who are empirical?

Some say, "It is miraculous,"
and others say "spectaculous,"
while others claim "ridiculous."

But there's the unexplainable
that some call "unsustainable"
and in the end's debatable.

Can what is unbelievable
ever be conceivable,
or just remain unthinkable?

12. Knowledge and Reason

To learn, a gift beyond compare,
for every child should not be rare.
To learn builds each child's self-esteem.
As knowledge grows, each child can dream.
Through knowledge each child's mind expands,
each learns of cultures, other lands.
As children learn to add, write, read,
their mother tongue meets a new need.
They speak and they communicate;
they learn with others to relate.
They then can build community
and serve the cause of unity.
The education of each child
alone prevents a world defiled
by ignorance and thoughtlessness,
stupidity, and carelessness.
Through wisdom we search in the soul
for wisdom to make humans whole.

13. Some People Think Too Much

Some people think too much
about themselves and such.
When they think just of self,
leave others on the shelf,
they won't be satisfied,
for all they have is pride.
Self-pride will not make friends
and never makes amends.
If you speak no kind word,
a kind word won't be heard.
If you know not to laugh,
who'll laugh on your behalf?
If you dare pay no mind
to others, you're not kind.
Your hallmark is ignore;
to others you're a bore.
Think of yourself much less;
your life then reassess:
grant others self-esteem,
which may your pride redeem.
The more you learn to share
yourself, others will care.

14. Innocent Simplicity

Innocent simplicity,
    an infant's gift at birth,
has an authenticity
    of priceless and rare worth.

Innocent simplicity
    is lost just as we grow.
Ours is full complicity;
    its loss we surely know.

And there's simple innocence,
    born of it unaware,
if we find it driven hence,
    it is a sad affair.

For innocence let us yearn
    as each of us matures.
From innocence let us learn
    it once was mine and yours.

15. Certainty of Knowledge

"I know for certain," may be said.
    "I really don't know," someone claims.
"I know it's true, that's what I read,"
    "I'm skeptical," said William James.

For James, known as a pragmatist,
    most surely valued reasoning.
By no means an abstractionist,
    he greatly valued listening.

To know with certainty is rare,
    to claim one knows without a doubt.
Can knowledge be beyond compare,
    if certainty leaves no way out?

In science there are proven facts
    that seem the root of certainty,
yet science often thus reacts—
    acknowledges there's mystery.

Of mystery what can one know,
    except that there is mystery?
It spurs us on to learn and grow,
    for facts indeed make history.

16. Certainty?

If there's no certain certainty
    which proves itself as true,
must I wait to eternity
    to know all that I knew?

If all that I thought that I knew,
    I could not ever know,
then there's no way to know what's true,
    existence is a show.

If there's not such a thing as fact
    that proves with verity,
how can I know how I should act,
    since there's no clarity?

17. Reality?

What are sheep with no shepherd
    and shepherds with no sheep?
If spotless were a leopard,
    has reason gone to sleep?

What if what we think is not
    the way things seem to be?
Reality, is it fraught
    with that which we don't see?

Hard, cold facts, oft hard to find,
    may be before our eyes.
Don't speculate, don't be blind;
    the facts do not despise.

SECTION 3

What Do You Have to Say about Matters of the Heart and Mind?

18. Mind and Heart

To educate the mind alone
    and to forget the heart
will penalize you when you're grown
    and tear your life apart.

The heart needs education too;
    it's sensitivities
need careful guidance through and through,
    no liabilities.

The heart and mind go hand in hand,
    there's knowledge that both need.
With both you'll better understand,
    therefore make this your creed:

Let mind and heart together grow
    in knowledge, and be free,
and make all those around you know
    a sweet philanthropy.

19. Moods

Our moods strike unexpected chords,
which do not always yield rewards.
When overjoyed have we concern
for some whose lives with hunger burn?
When we're depressed how can we see
the reasons to be filled with glee?
An apathetic mood is bad,
too lazy to be glad or sad.
A *laissez-faire* mood wants to be
for all free spirits the main key
to let them all do what they want,
and their bold acts to flaunt and flaunt.
Examine carefully each mood,
especially those that make you brood.

20. Decisions

Our rash decisions can cause harm
    to what we think and do.
Can we find inward an alarm
    to make our errors few?

We cannot all anticipate
    with a clairvoyant mind;
all our decisions can't abate
    all errors others find.

Results of what we may decide,
    if they bring others hurt,
with fairness will gravely collide.
    How can we hurt avert?

Ask first: Is my decision fair?
    Does it others involve?
Ask, should I this decision dare
    or quickly it dissolve?

21. Day Dreaming

Why do I wonder and day-dream?
Because things are not as they seem?
Because they could much better be?
Or is there something wrong with me?
I think of other worldliness.
Perhaps my thoughts are but a guess
at what might be or might make sense.
At times my thoughts are surely dense.
Of better times I want to dream
when folks are better than they seem.
When wisdom, talent, gifts are prized,
each person's value's recognized.
If this makes up my dreams to be,
perhaps I'll be a better me.

22. Winnowing

At harvest time one winnows grain
    to cast the chaff away.
The hardened kernels that remain
    make bread another day.

A winnowing we need in life
    to cast all chaff aside.
Winnow we may discomfort, strife,
    but does some chaff abide?

A winnowing good judgment needs,
    it needs no rush nor haste.
Good judgment with critique proceeds,
    so winnowing's no waste.

A winnowing of thoughts we need,
    a winnowing of speech,
a winnowing of every deed,
    for winnowing will teach.

A winnowing's a lifelong task;
    it's never finally done.
What will I in the morning ask?
    Has winnowing begun?

23. Poetry

What makes a poem, music sing?
Imagination is the thing!
The words and rhythms shape the art,
and various sounds then do their part.
Each culture organizes sound
quite differently the world around.
Some poetry is filled with rhyme
in couplets, triplets all in time.
Some poetry dismisses rhyme,
expressed in narrative sublime.
And music with inviting sounds
with diverse tempos, tones abounds.
Sometimes the music fits the text
and helps composers know what's next.

24. Creative Sensitivity

Creative sensitivity—
    Are artists with it born?
Or is it a proclivity
    for thoughts, forms yet unborn?

Does one learn creativity?
    Is somehow it innate?
Why is it such a mystery:
    some cannot, some create?

Can our environments affect
    how we learn to create?
Art offers what we least expect,
    when, where we can't dictate.

The disciplines of brush and pen,
    their practice some apply,
and other forms of art begin
    their wonders to supply.

Creative sensitivity
    needs practice to succeed.
Creative gifts, a mystery
    which often hopes exceed!

25. Alive Emotions

As water falls from giant heights
    and cascades over rocks and stones,
emotions rush with joys, delights
    through every sinew, to my bones.
The sudden joy of new love won
    or celebration of new birth:
a daughter or perhaps a son.
    I wonder: Can this be on earth?

But then a stark reality
    evokes emotions of contrast;
a darker side of things I see,
    the rushing waters churn so fast.
An overpow'ring waterfall
    of sadness floods my heavy soul,
as though this were my wailing wall.
    Can new love, births renew, make whole?

Can we emotions keep alive,
    the moments when our souls took flight?
The moments, no, but memories thrive,
    remembering to keep in sight
just how we felt, a touch, embrace,
    a silence or a spoken word.
Yes, those emotions we can trace
    how then we felt or what we heard.

26. Whence Happiness?

Whence comes the happiness we seek,
   from family, loved ones, things?
From life that's *bon vivant* or chic,
   from love that from hearts springs?

Is happiness something we find
   or something we create?
Can we to happiness be blind
   or happiness dictate?

Does happiness depend on us?
   Is it in our control?
Is it just something to discuss?
   Does happiness console?

Beware, beware, for happiness
   depends, depends on you.
Perhaps should we say, "more or less"?
   Would this be *déjà vu*?

Be *déjà vu* for everyone,
   for life is just that way?
We're happy if in the long run
   our good thoughts bad outweigh.

Our happiness is not acquired
    quite simply by good thoughts.
Our happiness must be desired
    but not by casting lots.

So much depends on attitude:
    to keep life's joys in view,
or happiness may you elude
    and happy days be few.

27. Human Loss

A moment one cannot forget,
    a first experience of death:
a loved one's loss that brings regret,
    the moment of one's final breath.

It is as though death stops all time,
    leaves emptiness within the heart;
and when it strikes life in its prime,
    life stops without the chance to start.

Death can be beautiful indeed
    when life is long, a life lived well.
A generous life, absence of greed,
    a memory to hold and tell.

SECTION 4

What Do You Have to Say about Truth?

28. Truth

In my youth,
I learned of truth.
Through the years
with all their tears,
I've known those,
who truth oppose.
In my eyes,
this is unwise,
for truth bears
all of life's cares.
One can trust
that truth is just.
Truth prevails,
when all else fails.
All must know:
falsehood forego,
Truth alone
can wrong atone.

29. Persistent Truth

There are few words that heal,
few words that make you feel
    that others care, if they deceive
    with lies, intrigue one can't believe.
Alternative the facts
every lie impacts
    the way some people act and think
    that brings a nation to the brink,

the brink of failure, lust,
the brink of loss, disgust.
    There's nothing that's lasting in lies,
    truth only so long bears disguise.
Persistent truth persists;
insistent truth insists.
    It outlasts lying and intrigue,
    for truth does not suffer fatigue.

30. If Truth Be Told

If truth is timeless and endures,
it's truth alone that falsehood cures.

Though truth endures and never dies,
it struggles constantly with lies.

The fact is this: truth never wins,
if one thinks truth and lies are twins.

They are related, to be sure;
just how this is, can be obscure.

One person tells the truth, she thinks,
another lies and never blinks.

Whom to believe with confidence—
for liars is there recompense?

But truth can be used to deceive
when only half's left to believe.

The whole truth, nothing more or less;
we're asked in court this to profess.

"If truth be told," we oft may say;
but caution—"if" may truth betray.

31. Truth Détente

Say something false, and then repeat;
    repeat it once again.
Put it on Facebook, and then tweet,
    the "truth" you're sure to gain.

For repetition is today
    the origin of "truth."
The truth becomes what you might say;
    objection is uncouth.

If someone says, "Tell me the truth,"
    what answer might you get?
What you were taught in prime of youth:
    "Truth should not facts forget."

Today with low regard for facts,
    which mean just what you want,
truth is achieved through mental acts;
    some call this truth détente.

32. The Art of Lying

To lie, an art, not born within,
    must first be learned or taught,
and those who lie find it no sin,
    unless, of course, they're caught.

Once Eve to Adam told a lie,
    the serpent first conceived,
but Adam did not blink an eye,
    though he had been deceived.

The art of lying with finesse
    through centuries has grown
till now we sadly ask, confess:
    Can true or false be known?

Among politicians today
    this highly treasured art
is used the heart of truth to slay!
    Can there be a fresh start?

If not, diplomacy is doomed,
    domestic, world concerns.
Will politicians new be groomed,
    who'll show that truth returns?

The world at large will go awry,
    if truth we cannot tell,
and human hearts will faint and die
    under the lying spell.

33. Dishonesty's Long Game

We mourn the loss of honesty,
and all the more integrity.
While politics succumbs to greed,
becoming rich is now its creed.
Manipulation's at its heart,
twisting the truth in every part:
confine the profits to the few
while poor folk know not what to do.
Deny the right to vote to those,
who crooked policies oppose.
One asks, "Is there not one soul left,
who is of selfish greed bereft?"
How can we start anew again
and break this vile, crass, ruthless chain?—
this chain of subterfuge and crime
and start again an upward climb
to heights of simple honesty
that's unafraid of bravery,
and like Odysseus hold fast
to hope of a return at last—
return at last to whence he came
to shed dishonesty's long game?

34. Narcissism Is Alive and Well

The facts of what takes place each day
    display life as it is,
but you the facts of life betray,
    if you just want to quiz,
to quiz with questions everything,
    regardless of what's true,
and let the truth mean anything,
    whatever would suit you.

You say, "I know what these facts mean.
    Another view is wrong,
No other meaning may you glean
    or can to truth belong."
Pleased with yourself and your own thought
    you create anarchy.
In narcissism's web you're caught
    and curse humanity.

35. Truth and Grace

What can exceed both truth and grace
    as values for our lives?
They filter words and deeds and trace
    the force that our lives drives.

Deception, lies, truth will expose;
    grace teaches to forgive.
The power-crazed truth will depose;
    grace shows new ways to live.

Though "truth" is such a simple word,
    how can one truthful be?
Refuse to say, "Truth is absurd."
    Seek truth's simplicity.

The word "grace"—it is simple too,
    but what then does it mean?
When some say, "I'll not forgive you":
    Forgive! Grace unforeseen.

Do "truth" and "grace" only define
    what suits your selfish will?
No, never think, "Truth/grace are *mine!*"
    or their effects you'll still.

36. Misunderstandings

Misunderstandings are a plague
    to many human relations.
When explanations are too vague,
    this creates tense situations.

Misunderstandings may be real,
    when facts we do not understand.
To careful study then appeal,
    for missing facts can be quicksand.

Misunderstanding: some may want
    the truth and facts thus to confuse.
Confusion then may others taunt,
    and leave them with distorted views.

Misunderstandings can cause loss
    of self-control, of piety.
Misunderstandings are the dross
    of fractures in society.

Misunderstandings clarify;
    save tension and anxiety.
Give voice to words like "verify,"
    "sobriety," "propriety."

SECTION 5

What Do You Have to Say about Caring?

37. Who Cares?

Is there no sense of childhood left?
Are children of childhood bereft?
Schools are no longer a safe place,
for guns and death invade their space.
Not ev'n on playgrounds are they safe
from drive-by shootings face to face.
Why birth a child who'll not be free,
for guns are daily on a spree
of death and injury in schools,
while politicians act like fools?
How can a child just be a child
when daily it's by guns defiled.
Will we let childhood vanish, die
because there is no will to try
to banish weapons made for war
from streets, and from our own front door?
Restore at least our children's rights
to childhood, not to guns and fights.

38. My Choice

Careless, caring, or carefree,
which one would I like to be?
Which of the three is my choice?
Caring always has my voice.
If I'm careless, I don't care;
if I care, then I'm aware
that I should care for others,
who are my sisters, brothers.
So if I would caring be,
that's how others will see me.

39. Be Thankful

Be thankful each day I am I,
lest I myself should wonder why.
Be thankful for rank poverty,
when no one cares if I am me?

Be thankful I am penniless
and worse that I am parentless?
Be thankful daily I'm alive,
and more that each day I survive?

"Be thankful"—something I must learn,
for thankfulness I cannot earn.
Be thankful, though life is unjust,
if I find someone that I trust?

Be thankful if life's circumstance,
gives those in poverty a chance.
Be thankful if I have been blessed,
if I can help those who're distressed.

Be thankful, I will try it out
perhaps it's best, without a doubt.
Be thankful I the source can be
of someone else's liberty!

40. Loneliness

In spite of social media
    so many people feel alone.
In spite of multi-media
    or every Android, new iPhone,

one finds the lonely everywhere.
    Though there is connectivity,
some folk will only sit and stare,
    resulting in passivity.

How can we find a remedy
    and loneliness eliminate?
Is there a worthwhile therapy
    or is it simply now too late?

The first step is to BE a friend,
    most surely this is no surprise
that friendship you cannot pretend;
    to BE a friend shows you are wise.

The time you spend with your iPhone
    resolve to spend with someone else.
You'll be surprised, you're not alone;
    the lonely feeling slowly melts.

41. Right and Wrong

What are the ways of right and wrong?
    For right it's simply do what's right.
The two will never get along.
    Each wants the other out of sight.

They both have ardent advocates.
    Though wrong will often rationalize,
the truth never negotiates.
    How true, the wrong truth never buys.

"There is no right, there is no wrong,"
    some nay-sayers are bold to say.
But justice won't just go along,
    with language that will lead astray.

Sometimes what's wrong or what is right
    is not as simple as it seems,
for those in pow'r let truth take flight
    and what is right is left to dreams.

Some justice systems qualify
    what is called wrong and what's called right.
But there's no way to justify
    deception and display of might,

display of might that takes away
    the rights of others, what they own.
Such acts will justice lead astray,
    as deadly seeds of wrong are sown.

Sow seeds of justice, sow what's right,
    let seeds of justice grow, bear fruit.
Then you will surely keep in sight
    the truth that will all wrong confute.

42. First Things First

First things first, we often hear,
    but who knows what comes first?
What's first for some is very clear,
    for others it's the worst.

On what criteria to decide?
    Do my concerns come first?
What principle will be my guide?
    Am I in self immersed?

If I love others the same way
    that I indeed love me,
this biblical idea might sway
    my actions thoroughly.

43. Worn Sad

I'm weary from a day worn sad
    by thoughts of tasks undone,
of opportunities I've had:
    a good deed for someone.

Of course, I'm filled with true lament,
    a feeling incomplete,
and I can never be content
    to suffer such defeat.

That's why a new day offers me
    a chance to start anew.
That's why I can't afford to be
    worn sad, just sad, and blue.

44. No Change

The times are few when I awake
    and feel the world's at peace.
As early dawn turns to daybreak,
    anxieties increase.

Not so, when I was just a boy,
    though World War 2 raged on.
I thought like those of ancient Troy:
    we won't be put upon!

Unlike in Europe's Nazi rage,
    war did not reach our shores,
and I played on at my young age
    inside and out-of-doors.

What if I'd been a boy in France,
    a boy in London-town?
I don't know if I'd had a chance
    when bombs came raining down.

And now at eighty-six I wake
    and still there is no peace.
At every moment of daybreak
    from war there's no release.

Yes, human nature's still beset
    with strange desires to crush
the lives, the lands of others yet,
    war gives humans a rush.

But boys and girls each day play on;
    it's therein that hope lies.
Their spirit can a new world spawn,
    so war-urge quickly dies.

45. Ingratitude

Soul's enemy ingratitude,
a dang'rous ego attitude,
is fostered oft by apathy,
the opposite of empathy.
Ingratitude erodes the soul,
on which it takes a drastic toll;
reflects insensitivity
and one's own crass proclivity
to put aside all one's concern
for others, friendliness to spurn.
Ingratitude or gratitude
decides how character is viewed.

46. Composure

Composure comes time and again
to those who're selfless and not vain,
to those who're thoughtful, ever kind,
who think beyond what's on their mind.

Composure should be our desire,
but some are trapped in mental mire
of their own selfishness and greed,
without concern for others' need.

Composure needs some quiet time,
our thoughts to filter and to prime.
Sit quietly, don't try to think
so body, soul, mind all can link.

Don't rush to think a useful thought,
sometimes such thoughts are simply caught.
Composure's there, awaits its turn;
composure's something all can learn.

47. Desires

Desires are such that they may wane,
but some desires themselves sustain.
Desires may never go away
both good ones, bad ones have their way.
Do our desires come from our need,
or do they just express our greed?
Desires sometimes resist control;
sometimes they will invade the soul.
Their grasp can be severely strong,
indeed may last one's whole life long.
Desires need genuine concern
the needs of others to discern.
For only when we see beyond
ourselves and things of which we're fond
will we control our strong desires,
as our humanity requires.

48. If Love is There

Round, round, and round the circle goes
of life that has me in its throes.
Sometimes there's scarcely time to see
all that transpires in front of me.
Like stormy winds that rush me by,
there's little time to know what's nigh.

A child is whisked from life by guns,
some parents lost, sisters, and sons.
The violence that takes some lives,
yes, makes me question, Who survives?
Where mothers, children suffer most,
war gladly is the welcome host.

But even amid death and gloom
we humans find for love there's room.
We stop, caress a child's soft hair,
just so she knows that love is there.
We kiss the lips of a loved one
and hug our children, every one.

There's nothing takes true love away;
with loss of life it seems that way.
But love that's genuine remains,
and generations long sustains.
Think constantly of love to share,
and others will know your love's there.

49. Love's Measure

Love's measure has no measure, hence
its meaning we cannot condense.
Is it to count throughout the day,
the times "I love you" that we say?
What of embraces, warm, sincere
and loving deeds and words of cheer?
A tender kiss, a soft held hand,
are these not ways to understand
if love is real and stands the test
so that one's love must not be guessed?
So many times we've known it so.
Yet without gestures, words we know
in silence and apart it's real,
for love we sense and love we feel.
Love rules emotions and the heart;
it's sensed in every sinew, part.
Our minds it also captivates,
unspoken thoughts it dominates.
Love's measure has no measure hence
its meaning we cannot condense.

50. Practice Patience, Master Fear

To practice patience, master fear,
    a challenge all must face;
ignore it and one's life is drear,
    moves at a dreary pace.

If one's impatient, knows no calm,
    and angry temper rules,
there is no magic, there's no balm;
    one's fool above all fools.

To be afraid takes many forms,
    and often conquers will.
One's spirit suffers inbred storms
    and cries out, "Peace, be still!"

To find such peace is a life quest,
    hence think of others first;
concern for others, a behest
    to lessen one's self-thirst.

Self-centeredness, impatience's food,
    quick tempers feeds, and fear.
To master fear it serves no good;
    its uselessness is clear.

To practice patience, master fear;
    beyond yourself begin
to think of others and adhere
    to love of self within.

51. A Human Curse?

The advent of all humankind,
    whenever it began,
    whatever the year span,
has left no one a peace of mind.

Invention of first human tools,
    the advent of the fire,
    to question, to inquire,
made human beings wise or fools.

With reading, writing came advance,
    ability to learn,
    acquire, as well as earn,
creating a strange circumstance.

For who would earn and who would learn?
    Would some folks be left out?
    O yes, without a doubt!
Societies' lasting concern.

For who would have and who have not?
    Who would be rich, who poor?
    The rich, richer for sure,
and keeping much more than they ought.

To learn to think of others first
    is not our first concern.
    When will this humans learn?
If never, humankind is cursed.

SECTION 6

What Do You Have to Say about Conflict?

52. U.S. Farm Workers

I looked across a field today
    to see farm workers at their toil.
The sun was hot and fields of hay
    so steamed with heat as if to boil.

The foreman's brazen, high-pitched voice
    barked English no one understood:
"Remember, folks, you have no choice,
    this is the way you'll do some good."

"You'll get your wages paid in cash,"
    still no one seemed to hear a word.
The foreman's looks were cold and brash,
    so he himself seemed quite absurd.

No word of Spanish did he say,
    that's why the workers paid no mind.
Illegal workers every day
    find they are always in this bind.

They're human beings, not Mex-trash,
    and farming here on them depends.
Without them U.S. farms would crash.
    It's time, it's time to make amends.

Treat them with honor, dignity,
    their language, culture dignify.
For them act with impunity;
    this U.S. farms can justify!

53. Economy and Poverty

Economy and poverty
    seem to go hand in hand,
and poor folk face adversity
    in every global land.

Consumer-planned economy
    based on supply-demand
can give the rich autonomy,
    the poor an empty hand.

This economic style or that
    cares not for poverty,
for profit is its main format
    and sometimes robbery.

Economies' grave consequence
    is they forget the poor.
They need a vital cognizance:
    wealth can the poor immure.

It's people in economies
    whose conscience is the key:
change systems from the enemies
    so needs of all we'll see.

54. A Daily Struggle

We humans struggle year on year,
    one day just to survive.
Too many struggle with the fear
    that they'll not be alive—
not be alive for lack of food
    from poor health and disease;
and sleeping on the street's no good;
    in winter pavements freeze.

But other folk live lavishly;
    their food waste is a crime.
They dress themselves quite garishly,
    care not to share a dime.
They pass the hungry on the street,
    in brand new, stylish cars.
They do not stop the poor to greet,
    when headed to the bars.

Do we think to make poor folk friends,
    invite them for a meal,
for apathy to make amends,
    a city's wounds to heal?
It's difficult to live this way
    for risk may be involved.
It's easier to stay away
    and leave this unresolved.

55. Conflict

I grew up in a southern town
    where schools were black and white;
where blue-laws often made folks frown,
    but kept the lid on tight.

Our churches too were white as snow,
    blacks, whites at their church prayed,
but as a child I did not know
    the evil churches made.

And then we moved to Birmingham,
    where I began to see
that segregation was a sham:
    for black folks and for me.

All water fountains "colored," "white"
    were marked for all to see.
The signs were large and in plain sight.
    One dare not disagree.

The big department stores were filled
    with white folks and with black.
Though black folks' money could be tilled
    but restrooms they did lack.

The city streetcars, busses too,
    had segregating signs.
This clearly showed a point of view
    which justice undermines.

This conflict is like no other,
    for Christ's words, I'd been taught:
you are to "love one another,"
    if you'd live as you ought.

Did Christians really this believe,
    I wondered: Can this be?
For Christ said, "I will *all* receive."
    And then said, "Follow me."

56. A Sheltered Past

Some days I'd like to be a boy
    of eight just one more time,
at Christmas time just one new toy,
    when chocolate cost a dime.

At Christmas time peace and good will,
    but racial wrong, no doubt;
injustice, and the poor and ill
    we rarely sang about.

Yes, I was sheltered in the past
    from racial hatred's crime.
I thought childhood would always last,
    and life would be sublime.

When I grew up I learned the truth
    that I had scarcely known
and slowly saw that in my youth
    I'd struggle, fight when grown.

I'd struggle then to right the wrongs
    ignored when I was young,
for justice to each soul belongs.
    I heard a new song sung.

Yes, "We shall overcome some day,"
    yes, we shall overcome,
though justice, prejudice delay
    equality for some.

But now I know there's no return
    to childhood and my youth.
No matter how for both I yearn,
    I face the glaring truth:

I grew up in a world white/black,
    a world not colorblind,
where black folks were under attack
    and daily were maligned.

A boy of eight I cannot be,
    a boy with blinders on.
Now I'm a man and I can see:
    to love we must be drawn.

57. Conversion[1]

I was converted, friends, last week;
    what an amazing change!
I used to think this made one weak
    and certainly, quite strange.
In church, this all did not take place,
    you never could guess where:
A football game brought face to face
    my sin with genuine care.

Our team lagged just two points behind;
    young Punkin' was our chance;
but we were in a dreadful bind!
    How could our team advance?
Our coach now had him on the bench.
    "Put Punkin' in," all yelled!
And then in me my racial grinch
    was once, forever quelled.

An African American end,
    the first on our ball team,
our coach then Punkin' in did send.
    It all was like a dream.

---

1. This poem is the author's recollection of a story told to him by a man who lived in a north Alabama town after the local high school had been integrated. The "I" refers to him, not the author. The name "Punkin" was the nickname of the African American football player on the team.

I'd never cheered a black before.
    Then Punkin' caught the ball,
and scored from fifty yards or more.
    Our loss he did forestall.

With prejudice, I had been filled
    for all my years, lifelong,
"Put Punkin' in," my fears had stilled
    as I joined with the throng.
Yes, this is how conversion works;
    you are transformed by truth:
gross prejudice the spirit irks,
    from views learned in your youth.

Conversion means there's dignity,
    that you have learned to share
instead of gross inequity
    which prejudice lays bare.
I learned this at a football game,
    when I cheered Punkin' on.
I shed my prejudice and shame:
    my prejudice was gone!

58. Do Unto Others—What?

The era of the civil rights
    I lived through as a young, white man.
There were some terrible street sights,
    when folks from German shepherds ran,
and firehouse hoses struck them hard
    with streams of water packed with power,
and no one could from danger guard;
    police arrests made hour by hour.

I lived in Birmingham, AL,[2]
    Bull Connor's realm of violence,
which made the streets a living hell
    without a chance of recompense.
Some members of the KKK
    blew up a church on 16th street;
to kill black girls, they thought OK,
    and justice was nowhere to greet.

Non-violence was met with hate;
    I saw this clearly with my eyes.
At UAB[3] no, no debate.
    "Let Arthurine[4] in" one sign cries.

---

    2. Pronounce the letters A and L.
    3. University of Alabama. Pronounce each letter: U, A, B.
    4. Arthurine Lucy was the first African American student applicant at the main campus of U.A.B in Tuscaloosa, AL.

George Wallace, governor, says, "No!
    Right here is where I take my stand.
It's somewhere else she'll have to go.
    Divided, equal is our brand!"

Today the cries for justice rise
    from many folk, white, black, and brown,
from Asians too, it's no surprise:
    "Our cry for justice don't strike down!"
Racism's still alive and well:
    another black man's lost his life.
Now from the streets a peaceful swell:
    "Just give us justice, no more strife!"

Throughout my life I've seen it all:
    The cries for justice that brought change,
Now cries for justice that us call
    to stop racism; is that strange?
Police brutality lives on
    against the folks with colored skin.
The streets cry out from night till dawn
    "Yes, black lives matter"—all are kin.

Now do to others as you would
    all other folk should do to you!
What if police this premise could
    let change the course of what they do?
Each neighborhood might also change,
    the served and server might be friends.
This might be, though some think it strange,
    an answer that could serve all ends.

59. In Birmingham

I went to school in Birmingham
    in grades six, sev'n, eight, nine,
where whites had a defined program
    to keep the blacks in line.

Our school was white, no blacks allowed,
    and our school day began
with prayer when all our heads were bowed,
    as if all were God's plan.

We pledged allegiance to our flag,
    some with a southern drawl;
I later knew the troubling snag:
    we said, "justice for all."

"Justice for all" did not exist,
    I learned as years went by,
for segregation did persist,
    ev'n caused black folk to die.

When school was out, the large playground
    was where we played kickball.
Some white and black boys gathered 'round
    awaiting for the call

to choose our sides, mixed black and white;
    our eyes were on the game.
The best team's what we had in sight—
    to play the game our aim.

Some black boys were of my own age
    and also lived nearby.
With no ill feelings to assuage,
    we gave kickball a try.

I never thought that I'd look back
    and say, "We had it right,"
for whether we were white or black
    we joined in with delight.

I guess if the police had seen
    us playing at the school,
they'd stopped us, made an awful scene
    and called each one a fool.

Oh, I remember life back then
    with joy and with regret;
my recourse now is with my pen
    to help pay white's man debt.

60. Justice and Mercy

When justice, mercy dare to meet,
then kindness, fairness one may greet.

When justice, mercy do not meet,
then kindness, fairness know defeat.

If justice, fairness we dare wed,
most likely there'll be less blood shed.

Though justice, mercy are not twins,
when joined together, hope begins.

If justice, mercy are close friends,
then right and good to all extends.

When justice, mercy show we care,
it is as if we pray a prayer.

This prayer is prayed for humankind:
"Let justice all with mercy find."

61. Lost Humanity?

The Alabama prisons fail
    to simply be humane;
They sanctify a word like "jail,"
    a sacredness insane.

"Parole" becomes the kind of word
    that inmates should not hear.
For simplest crimes parole's unheard,
    and ev'n when death is near.

A woman inmate of long years
    is at the point of death;
ev'n so, the parole board just sneers.
    Its "No" seals her last breath.

In human nature there's desire
    to make wrong-doers pay.
But prisoners need not acquire
    the right to just, fair play.

Does crime mean that you forfeit life,
    forfeit humanity?
A convict's simply a low-life
    for an eternity?

Some fight to protect embryos
    still in a mother's womb;
but saving the same life oppose,
    if it commits crime—doom!

Yet Christians, Muslims, also Jews
    know well the word "forgive,"
a word not in parole boards' views,
    yet rule if/how pris'ners live.

Humanity's a gift at birth,
    some think—God-given right.
But human beings 'cross the earth
    play God from dawn till night,

for they decide who goes to jail
    and how long this may be,
and they decide if there is bail,
    and if someone goes free.

62. Which Way Humankind?

Wherever humankind is found,
    there's love and there is hate.
Wherever humankind is bound,
    it may arrive too late,

too late to remove prejudice,
    too late to show one's care,
too late for lies and cowardice,
    too late to do what's fair.

Can humankind then change its ways?
    Can humankind repent?
Can humankind truth, honor praise,
    for honesty be spent?

Collectively there's no reply,
    except as folk unite.
Each person can with truth ally,
    then humankind's a light,

a light to everyone to do
    what's true and what is just,
a light that guides both me and you
    to live the way we must.

63. Equality & Justice for All

To segregate and isolate
    after the Civil War
became the way to legislate,
    create the cultural core
of many of the southern states
    for decades yet to come,
where racism still perpetrates
    life that proceeds therefrom.

The movement known as Civil Rights
    brought progress, to be sure,
but many still defend the whites
    and want no cultural cure.
Still there are those who justice prize,
    fight for equality,
while others simply close their eyes,
    lapse into lethargy.

The U.S. claims "justice for all,"
    ignores it yet at will.
Indeed, this is its great downfall;
    it does so with great skill.
In Israel apartheid reigns
    or segregation plus,
for Palestinians "live in chains."
    Their rights?—do not discuss!

Our U.S. government supports
    Israel every year
with billions in aid, per reports,
    though rights just disappear.
Though segregation we oppose
    at home, why not abroad?
Democracy is Israel's pose,
    but is it there a fraud?

Apartheid and segregation,
    are basically the same.
The new name a "Jewish Nation"
    excludes non-Jews by name.
The name is Palestinian—
    no human rights, no land.
Whatever your opinion,
    for justice take a stand!

One cannot Hamas' actions bless,
    by occupation primed.
More violence is an abscess—
    for peace efforts ill-timed.
Fight violence with violence
    the usual human way,
but violence has no recompense
    except with death to pay.

America, hypocrisy
    is written on your face,
for to the term "democracy"
    your actions bring disgrace.

Apartheid or segregation
    oppose, yes, in your land,
but do not support a nation
    that will not take this stand!

Index of Subjects and Names

Adam, 45
African American, xix, 83, 85
artist, 33

caring, vi, x, xvii–xviii, 54
Christian, xix, 80, 91
Cicero, xiv, 4
civil rights, 85, 93
composure, vii, 64

death, 12, 37, 53, 66, 90, 94
dignity, xix, 9, 76, 84

emotion, vi, x, xiii, xv, xviii, 34, 67
Eve, 45

fear, vii, xviii, 68–69, 78, 84
friend, iv, x, xvii, 9, 19, 56, 63, 78, 83, 86, 89

guns, 53, 66

happiness, vi, 35–36
honor, xix
humanity, vii, x–xi, 12, 48, 65, 90–91
humankind, vii, 70–71, 89, 92

ingratitude, vii, 63
Israel, 93–94

James, William, 21
Jew, 91, 94
justice, vii, xx, 57–58, 80–82, 85–87, 89, 93–94

Keats, John, xiv, 4
Kimbrough, S T, Jr., ix–xi

loneliness, vii, 56
love, vii, x–xi, xiv, xviii–xix, 9, 12–13, 34–35, 37, 59, 66–67, 69, 80, 82, 92

Muslim, 91

narcissism, vi, x, 48
Nazi, 61

Odysseus, 47

Palestinian, 93–94
patience, vii, x, xviii, 68–69
peace, 9, 61, 68, 70, 81, 86, 94
poetry, vi, xiii, 11, 32
poor, xvii, xix, 47, 70, 77–78, 81
poverty, vii, xvii, xix, 55, 77
pray, 13–14, 79, 89
prayer, xx, 87, 89
prejudice, x, 8, 12, 82, 84, 92

racism, xix, 86, 93

sadness, 34
segregation, xi, 79, 87, 93–95
Shakespeare, William, xiv, 4
Shelley, Percy Bysshe, 6

thankful, vi, xvii, 55
truth, vi, xvi, 8, 10–11, 39, 41–50, 57–58, 81, 84, 92

Wallace, George, 86
Watson, J. Richard, v, xi
Word War, 2, 61

www.ingramcontent.com/pod-product-compliance
Lightning Source LLC
Chambersburg PA
CBHW071713040426
42446CB00011B/2049